LIGATURE OF EMOTIONS

POETRY COMES FROM THE HEART AND REACHES THE SOUL

UTKARSH BAJPAI

Om Shri Ganeshaya Namah

With the blessings of Lord Ganesha, this book is dedicated to my family and well-wishers, who always stood beside me as a pillar of motivation and supported me in my tough times.

I would also like to dedicate this book to all the readers, who still have faith in true love.

Let's keep on uplifting humanity and spreading love.

Contents

Contents

Foreword

I am delighted and honoured to write the foreword to this poetry book named- "**Ligature Of Emotions**", written by my esteemed and very good friend Utkarsh Bajpai. I still remember when he showed me his first poetry a while back, I immediately thought that book is going to be a house full of emotions and it has turned out just that. His poetry presentation and writing style is the word easy to be understood, the composition of poetries in this book is the manifestation of emotions via thoughts via words onto paper, in simple words, it is the conveyance of ordinary words into others, more poetic words, whilst the reader is confronted with the task to re-establish the origin of metaphoric references. I personally suggest all the readers read this book with their hearts so that they may feel the power of words. I convey my best wishes for the book and hope it turns into a bestselling book soon.

- Dr Lorna Abvarado (Linköping University, Sweden)

Preface

Poems have always been the source of inspiration from ancient times. Poems describe the real beauty of an object in its own oriented manner. Poetry and imagination are two different sides of the same coin. In order to write a perfect piece of poetry, one needs to have a clear vision. Poems are expressions of mixed feelings and these are one of the ancient arts, and it begins as did all the fine arts, within the original wilderness of the earth. This book is a collection of poems written by the author to reflect the zeal of emotions, hidden inside the heart of true Lovers. In order to feel the flow of emotions, kindly read this book using your heart, so that my words can touch your Soul. As an author of this book, I ensure that book will act as an eternal graffiti written in the heart of its readers.

- Utkarsh Bajpai (Author and Poet)

Acknowledgements

I believe that writing a book is quite harder than I thought and more rewarding than I could have ever imagined. This book would haven't been possible without the support of my family. They always stood by me during every struggle and all my successes. I'm eternally grateful to my Maa and Papa, who took in an extra mouth to feed when they didn't have to. They taught me discipline, tough love, manners, respect, and so much more that has helped me to succeed in life.

Whatsoever I am today is due to the blessings of my parents and the love of my sister. I thank them for playing a very special role in my life. I do believe that my words won't be enough to thank them for their gratitude but would like to dedicate this book to them as a token of respect. I would also like to thank all my teachers, who always acted as true mentors for me, during my school and college days, you all are the real heroes of my life who trusted my dreams and skills, Thank you, teachers, for your guidance and motivation. Last but not least I would also like to thank the musketeers of my life: Abhishek, Farhan, Akash and Digesh for their support and belief in me, and for giving meaning to my life.

Prologue

Significance of Poetry in Human Life

Poetry is not just the string of words,
It's a ligature of Emotions that ties the heart and soul together.
Poetry is not just the phrases to pen down,
It is a zeal of emotions which can only be felt.
Poetry is written from the heart and touches the soul,
It brings out all the secrets when you write more and more.
Poetry describes the world in its oriented manner,
It acts as an inspiration to bring out the hidden imagination.
Poetry lets your heart speak out the truth,
And express all your desire in a written manner.
Poetry is not just the string of words,
It is only the Ligature of Emotions.

1. Dear Maa

When I was small,
You were always there to take my care.
You took me out of every danger
and protected me as a guardian angel.
You are the one who stands for me
when there was no one.
In the sands of time,
There are your footprints in my life.
You are the only one who guided me,
When there was none.
You showed me the right path,
Whenever I was standing at the crossway of my life.
You are the ray of hope
whenever all my ideas are getting flop.
You are the one who holds my hand
and makes me upright to stand.
You taught me to face the world,
with my hard work and struggle.
Whenever I suffer from loneliness,
I memorise all your teachings and lessons.
You are the role model in my life,
So I can be a model for other's life.
Achievements which I have got in life,
It's not only my hard work.

But your teachings converted,
my hard work into a successful Life.

2. Dear Papa

In the pathway of my life,
You are the source of motivation for me.
Whenever I was there in the midst of darkness,
I found you who acted as burning candlelight for me.
You are the one who always stood beside me
When I was in need of someone.
As I recall the memories of my childhood,
I found you making me upright to stand.
You are the one who taught me to walk,
And took my care in every daring layer.
You are the source of enthusiasm for me,
And you also acted as a storehouse of motivation for me.
You play different roles in my life,
Sometimes you act as atm for me,
Sometimes you act as a banker for me,
Sometimes you act as a teacher for me,
But every time you took special care of me.
I am thankful to God for giving me a father like you,
So that I can prove to be a good son for you.
I promise you from the core of my heart,
That I will never let you down.

3. Dear Sister

Dear sister you know you are my first friend,
A friend with whom I fight a lot.
But I also know that you are the one who loves me a lot,
And how much you argue you can not be drawn apart.
You are the best gift I ever received from god,
You are the friend who brings me out of difficult times.
And you are my partner in all the crimes,
You are the one with whom I laugh and smile.
And may these memories never be relinquished from my heart until I die.
You are the companion with whom I can express my thoughts and feelings,
You are the one who protected me from getting bored in family dealings.
Dear sister when you are on my side,
The world seems to be filled with joy and life.
But when you are not around,
Days are full of strife.
I still remember you took my care when I was suffering badly from covid19,
You protected me as a shield, so that I may not feel alone and weak.
You consulted doctors and got me medicated to protect me from the disease,
Your efforts protected my life,
And made me disease free.
I never had any words to thank you,

But I must admit my dear sister, you are the most precious gift of my life.
Never consider yourself all alone,
Because I will be standing as a google map in all the crossways of life.
I will protect you from all darkness,
And will always be your guiding light.

4. Dear Future Wife

I love you the way you are,
More beautiful and dazzling than stars.
A sense of euphoria grips me from head to toe
When you enter my dreams and make them true.
You will be the queen in the kingdom of my heart,
and then I will be the king so we will never be apart.
I will be the warrior to fight for our love,
So that I will be your wall and shield you from all danger.
You will be my majesty,
and I will take care of you forever.
You will be my destiny
and will leave you never.
I will wipe all your tears,
and always make you smile.
You are not just another girl to me,
because you are the love of my life.

5. My First Love

The girl whom I love,
Lives in my dream.
She is not yet present,
But alive in my dreams.
When I see her Face,
It provide a sparking charm in me.
When she comes close to me,
It provides me with all plans she have for me.
When I touch locks of her hair,
Her smile unlocks all my dare.
She is the only one whom I believe in,
And the one with whom I want to live in.
Your presence in my dreams makes me uncomfortable,
And your absence makes me intolerable
When I look into your eyes,
I get lost in my own world of mine.
But when I come out of it,
There was not a single drop of wine.
But still I feel addicted of your eyes,
Which embeds me to get lost in the beauty of your eyes.
When I come down to her lips,
To feel the spring of the first kiss.
But as the time passed by,
All the attempts goes to wane.

She ignores all my trials,
By applying unsuitable conditions of the time.
Because my dream was broken and it was a morning Nine.

6. Love Story

When I heard it the first time,
What love is?
I realised it is just a mess,
It ruins two hearts,
Which is none other than suffering hours.
I was Eighteen,
When first embedded in love.
I used to spend days and hours with my love,
But time ditched me and distance took us apart.
As the wheel of time passed by,
We both were in our twenties of life.
My love for her was invincible,
And it kept on increasing with each day passing by.
Her dreams made me unstable,
Usually after every midnight.
In my dreams, we talk a lot,
And share our feeling each and every time.

7. Sensation Of My Heart

Whenever In Dreams I see you,
I found myself to be lost in you.
You seem to be the sensation of my heart,
But in you every time I see a piece of new art.
Your beauty is like an art to me,
Which is filled wid the colour of mine.
You are the cented candle to me,
And I am your burning light.
You are the source of inspiration to me,
When I could not see the single sight.
You just guide me the path to success,
Whenever I was In cross way of my life.
Whenever I am in pains and suffering,
I just think of you and all my mess goes off my life,
Your memories are an asset to me.
Which is a very important part of my life
Why the hell you stay away from me?
When you are the special part of my life.
Your dreams makes me unstable to sleep,
Which distrubs the working of my life.
Even the can of beer is not enough,
To take your memories out of mind.
I just tried and tried again,
To just forget that amazing night.

When I promised to be yours,
And you promised to be mine.
Then what happened to that shit,
It is not working anymore.
The Hand of the clock passed by,
But your memories are never lost by.
I will think of you again and again,
Till the last breath of my Life.

8. That Wintry Night

It was a snowy wintry night,
When I saw you in blur light.
Your beauty was quite shaddy to me,
But you were looking damm beautiful in that moonlight.
The Trafficking of snow was on,
But the sensation of my heart was going off.
Your beauty was filling adoring temptation in me.
And I was totally gone off.
The moon was high up in the sky,
It seems it was shining for last night.
It was like a dream night to me,
Because for a lover It's love at a first sight.
The dream was unbelievable to me,
As it was a very daring night.
I was totally lost in her beauty,
As it was just the beginning of family life.
The Storms were thundering,
The lightings were quite high.
But still I remember,
That I was standing for you in that wintry night.

9. Darkness of Night

The darkness of your eyes,
Is like a night without a moonlight.
I think of you each morning,
And dream of you every night.
The murmuring of your pink lips,
Makes me unstable usually after midnight.
I just only think of your arms around me,
And can not express my delight.
The sensation of your touches,
Burns a fire in my mind.
Then temptation of my heart,
Touches the height of the Sky.
I have never fallen for someone before,
But now I think it's a right time.
I think it's time for me to be yours,
and yours to be mine.
I Just swear in name of god,
I just think of you in the darkness of night.

10. What If

What if our story becomes a past?
What if our memory gets diminished?
What if we have to suffer in life?
But my love for you will be always infinite.
What if the night is dark?
What if there is not a single path?
What if the time is against us?
But I promise no one can separate us.
What if you are away from me?
What if we can not meet today?
What if you are beyond my reach right now?
What if my heart gets broken every time when I feel of you?
But Every time I say we will meet one day, did you hear we will surely meet one day.

11. Temptation For You

I remember the first look you gave me,
I wasn't sure what to do.
I was unaware of the feelings,
But it was something different something good.
I was behaving in an unusual manner,
But it was expected in that situation.
I was lost in your beauty,
Which shooked me up in every condition.
I remember the first time I felt jealous of you,
The feeling was foreign but something new.
Blinding anger that made no sense,
Because I want you and only you.
I want no guy beside you,
Because I only want you and you are mine.

12. Love At First Sight

When I saw you for the first time,
That sight filled an adorable temptation in my heart.
You were the mentor of the class,
And I was sitting at the last.
You were looking damn pretty in that blue school uniform,
Alas! I was stuck in your charm.
I was lost in own Disney world of mine,
When I saw you for the first time.
I was quite mad at dreaming about you,
Your presence in my thoughts keeps me stuck in you.
When I imagine you usually at night,
It burns a fire of temptations in my mind.
I just think of you day and night,
And try to write for you in the lamp light.
You became an inseparable part of my life,
When I saw you for the first time.
When I memorise your face today,
That golden nose ring is still present in my mind.
Which brings out an attractive charm in you,
When I saw you for the first time.
It may be the tale of years ago,
But I still remember every line.
You may be far away from me ,
But your pressence is always there in my mind.

This may not be the end of this love story,
Because I still remember when I saw you for the first time

13. Love Is My Life

Love is just not a word,
It's just an assembly of fire within in our heart.
Love is not a thing you get lot and lot,
But truly love the girl you have got.
Love can not be killed and it never dies,
It can be just transferred from your heart to mine.
Love is so sweet and so kind,
I just love the girl who is there in my soul and mind.
Love is always there to take care of you,
The feelings which I can say are so true.
My love for you is not a game,
It's so pure and lively as I take your name.
My love is my life,
I can't wait for a day to make my love my wife.
*Therefore I can be with her 24*7 day and night,*
So that there can be no further darkness in my life.

14. Valentine's Day

Today is the day of romance,
Today is the time for me to be yours and yours to be mine.
Today is a day when everyone is trying to win someone's heart,
And hope there doesn't fall apart.
Today I would also reveal the fire within my heart,
So that you may explore the vault of my soul and heart.
You were the most beautiful dream of my life,
Which I see every day and night.
Today I try to make you mine,
So now I ask you the question that seems to be very fine.
So just I want to ask you from the core of my heart,
Will you be always mine?

15. Dear Would-be Wife

Today is the new beginning of our life,
We both are together forever as a single soul of Husband and wife.
Our togetherness is a beautiful creation of god,
Which describes his presence a lot.
God granted us the gift of togetherness,
So that we may set the example of love for all.
Words are just not enough today,
When our love will show the way.
I wish to share our lives together,
To build a special plan forever.
Down the road walk side by side,
And just see each other with a smile and pride.
Today is the day that will change and transform our life,
When I have to live with my beautiful and lovely wife.
Thus this day is the union of two hearts,
Together we agree till death do us apart.

16. May I

May I hold Your hand forever,
And never let you go.
May I bring back your smile,
And never let you cry.
May I love you from the core of my heart,
So that no one can separate us apart.
May I be your man,
Who loves you the most and live for you till the end.
May I vow to be true and faithful to you,
So that I can freely love you.
May I look into your dark black eyes,
So that I can lose myself in you.
May I pull you close to my heart and whisper in your ear,
So that I may reveal my feelings and plans without any fear.
May I write many more rhymes,
To prove my love every time.
May I reveal what I do every day,
Think of you and spending my whole life loving in the darkness of midnight.

17. Do Love Exist

Do the fairy really exist,
This was a question when I saw you for the first time,
You behaved like another girl to me,
But you don't know you are my life.
Do the heart stop beating,
This was the second question that arose in my mind.
I just smiled at my emotions and said it's a feeling of love my friend,
Now you have to survive with this for a lifetime.
Do the words required for expressing,
Was a seriouslydoubtful question to my mind.
I just wrote your name in my heart,
And the feeling of love and desire arose in my mind.
Do the distance matter,
Was a confusing question to me.
My heart smiled and said when she is in me,
Then how she can be far away from your eyes.
Do the involvement of the past is necessary,
When you are in love with a real guy.
I promise you that from my soul and heart,
I won't let your past to make you cry.
Do anything else required to prove my love to you,
My feelings for you will never change.
Good time may come and go but I will be standing always by your side,
Just remember one thing Utkarsh will always love you for a lifetime.

18. HeartBeat

When ever I close my eyes,
Your face strikes my Mind.
Your beauty is so true and pure,
As god itself created you as a heartbeat of mine.
When ever you come in my dreams,
The love you give defines me.
I think of you day and night,
And love you till the last breath my life.
I love you more than anyone,
I just had to let you know.
My feelings for you will never change,
And I will never let you go.
What ever pains it take,
But I will prove my love every time.
I accepted you as my better half,
Now its your turn to be mine.

19. Spark Of Love

In the darkness of midnight,
Your beautiful face act as moonlight.
I always think of you every second and every time,
And your dreams come into my sleep each night.
I really miss you in every part of my time,
And I hope you would be missing me too in your life.
A spark of love is burning in your heart,
Then why the hell do you stay apart.
I would say that,
I really love you yaar.
I know you can push me away,
But I will come back for you every time.
Sometimes I try to hate you,
But it's not more than an hour.
I will do everything I can to get closer to you
And wait for you till the last hour.
So I suggest you remember that,
I love you till my death is a fact of my heart.

20. I Do Promise

I do promise to cherish and love you,
And my love is unconditional without any doubt.
I do promise to treasure our friendship and care for you,
Today, tomorrow and forever with my pure heart.
I do promise to trust and honour you,
Till my last breath do us apart.
I do promise to laugh and cry with you,
Until I take all your pain apart.
I do promise to stand by you through good times or bad,
And never let you suffer them all alone.
I do promise to be faithful and loyal to you,
So that I may feel privileged of sharing my life with you.
I do promise to have no greater love than you,
So that I can only pamper and love you.
I do promise to accept you as the greatest gift of my life,
And onlylove you, again and again, each day passing by.

21. If You Are Mine

If you are my breath,
Then I would be your soul.
Together we live,
And never let you go.
If you are my rose,
Then I would be your sun.
Painting you in a rainbow,
When the rain comes.
If you are my moon,
Then I would be your light.
To shine with you,
To make a romantic night.
If you are my fate,
Then I would be your destiny tonight.
Caressing your shores,
Soft and gentle I would be.
If you are my land,
Then I would be your sea.
Your constant companion,
Which makes a mesmerizing scene.
If you are mortal,
Then I would be your love divine.
My devotion for you is eternal,
To you my lovely valentine.

22. Let Me

Let me be on your side,
To take care of your broken heart.
Let me fix every single piece with my love,
And wipe your tears apart.
Let me heal all your wounds,
And fill your life with a beautiful smile.
Let me bring you up the mountain's peak,
And let you touch the skies.
Let me remind you of the beauty,
When I look into your beautiful eyes.
Let me promise to love you for every moment of forever,
And when everything else crumbles I will never.
Let me fly with you my beautiful one,
It's time we leave the past.
Let me share our life together to build a special plan forever,
Down the road walk side by side,
To see each other with a smile and pride.
Let me be your armour to protect you from all harm,
Like you do for me with a lucky charm.
Let me hold your hand and take this oath in the name of God,
I will be on your side till the death do us apart.

23. Queen Of My Heart

Whenever you looked at me,
It adds a zeal of an emotion in me.
Which fires a temptation of love in my heart,
That will never keep you apart.
Whenever you smile at me,
The person in me rapidly falls in love with you.
He is the one who can sail any sea,
All of that he would do just for you.
Whenever you come close to me,
It ignites a fire in my mind.
The murmuring of your pink lips,
Makes me unstable usually after midnight.
I think of your arms around me,
And can not express my delight.
Whenever I see you,
It's always love at first sight.
To you, I give the whole me,
For I believe that you are my destiny.
I want to offer you, my soul,
So that my queen I will be all yours.

24. Togetherness(Dedicated to Mom & Dad)

Your togetherness is a beautiful asset of God,
Which describes his presence a lot.
He moulded you both with his own presence,
So that you can fulfil his presence in all.
He granted you the gift of togetherness,
So that you may set an example for all.
He created you both together to share each other life,
So that you may help each other to face all the obstacles of life.
You both look complete together,
May heaven showers his blessings forever.
Always stand for one another in life,
And support each other in struggles of the time.
Let the time pass by,
But your togetherness should never be lost by.

25. Should I

Should I spend some time with you?
Should I write some lines for you?
Should I open all the doors of my heart?
And would never let you stay apart.
Should I consider you as my soul?
And never allow you to go.
Should I take the privilege of being your man?
And stand by you till my end.
Should I show you your beauty from my eyes?
One that only real love can have.
Should I kiss your forehead?
And make you blush with a smile.
Should I hold you for a while?
And lost myself in you, my dear lifeline.
Should I replace your past?
And make you mine for a lifetime.
Should I vow to be faithful and loyal to you?
And I promise to be always available for you.
Should I look into your dark black eyes?
And I promise never to tell you lies.
Should I pull you close and whisper in your ears?
And tell you my feelings without any fear.
Should I pull out my heart to prove my love?
So that you may be convinced and would become my wife.

26. Stolen Heart

I always tried so hard for you,
I always gave my best.
I gave you all I have,
And now there is nothing left.
You came as a dream come true,
And you just stole my heart.
Then tore it into two parts,
And now I am feeling apart.
If you are the land of my life,
Then I would be your sea.
Your constant companion,
Without you, I don't make any mesmerising scene.
I have been divided by your decisions,
And confused by your words.
Now I am burning in the fire full of tempted desire,
All turned to ashes and now there is nothing left.
I am living in the present,
My mind is on the past.
Not knowing what I will lose.
Not knowing what will last.
I am blinded by fear,
And drowning in doubt.
I am struggling to be free,
And just looking for a way out.

I always tried so hard for you,
I always gave my best.
I gave you my all,
And now there's nothing else left.

27. Yaarana

Whenever I was screwed in mess,
I know you will be taking me out of that hell.
You have been always there for me,
Through the good times or bad.
I know I can count on you,
Because I know you will be always there when I am sad.
Whenever I had a bad day,
I know that you are only a call away.
Whenever in life there are crazy turns,
I know you are always there to help me and learn.
You are a source of motivation for me,
Whenever I face a dead end.
We have shared so many good memories together,
And I know in all my problems there was always your share.
My life without you just would not be right,
And I know you will be always there to guide me at every sight.
I know we will be best friends forever,
And we will be together till the end.
You always kept our friendship ahead of everything,
that's why you are there in the core of my heart my friend.

28. What's the Need Of Fear?

Doubt comes to my mind,
Why live a life of wild?
Just be yourself and keep fear out of you,
Because fear can not be your destiny, my friend.
Life is full of joy and happiness,
Then what's the need for fear my friend.
Fear resides in the past of you,
So forget it and have a sip of dew.
Just take a stand and boost yourself,
And kick the ass of fear again.
Just improve your thoughts and control your destiny,
There is no need of fear in you my friend.
Live your life as you die tomorrow,
Because life is not given back again.

29. You are a warrior

You are a warrior,
You are not weak.
Your valour is high,
Like a mountain's peak.
Your bravery is not a fairy tale,
Your struggles are crammed into chronicles of time.
And you will be always remembered,
As an inspiration for all mankind.
You are a warrior,
Don't let your guards down.
You are a champion and born to win,
So never put yourself down.
Don't let the cloud of doubt arise,
Within the four walls of your mind,
Your sword is sharp and your sheild is strong,
Tear that might enemy which lets you down.
You are a warrior,
Comeout like a decorated soldier.
Don't be a prisoner of war, my friend,
You are a warrior, born to win.
Your struggles are hard,
And wounds are bloody and deep.
You are a wounded lion,
Fearless and ready to hunt like a warrior king.

30. Glory of My Land

I belong to the land of Vedas,
Where the civilisation was ancient and early.
I belong to the land whose feet are touched by the Indian Ocean,
Which is named after its glory.
I belong to the land of Ganges,
Where the rivers are holy.
I belong to such a land,
Where honour and respect are given to every living being.
I belong to the land of cultures,
Where the religions are true and friendly.
I belong to the birthplace of gods,
The land is blessed and holy.
I belong to the land where martyrs are born,
So that Indian try colour may never be bent down.
I belong to the land which won countless wars,
Just to maintain peace for you all.
I belong to the most peaceful place in this world,
The land of hind is my home and I am an Indian.

31. I miss you

Memories we share are an important part of my life,
Which makes me uncomfortable usually after midnight.
While sleeping I look at each bright star,
And think about what you are doing. and where you are?
We were separated several years ago,
But my heart does not allow you to go.
I am deeply sad and lonely without you,
But I try not to let it show.
Whenever I sleep, I only think of you,
You might be gone for now but the memories I will always keep till death do us apart.

Author's Bio

Hi, I'm Utkarsh Bajpai and I am hailing from Manchester of East, i.e., Kanpur City in the state of Uttar Pradesh. I am passionate about writing. I take pleasure in immersing myself in learning about new and exciting areas. I consider myself a person who is creatively oriented, thus writing allows me to use my imagination and express myself creatively. And over the years, I have developed several skill sets that are essential for writing such as poetry writing or Short-stories writing.

My journey in the domain of writing started with the publishing of my research papers in several international Journals and at this stage, I wanted to learn more about analytics and content strategy, also one of my books named: "**Proficiency in Computer Applications with the concept of Java**" is published by Amazon Kindle publication and is sold worldwide. This achievement boosted the fire of confidence in my life. Currently, I am working as a chairperson of **Cawnpore Computers Private Limited** but when I am free, I enjoy cooking and travelling the world.

Don't forget to connect with me on:

- **Instagram:** https://www.instagram.com/kanpuriya_boy/
- **Facebook:** https://www.facebook.com/kanpuriyaboy
- **Twitter:** https://twitter.com/kanpuriyaboy
- **Linkedin:** https://www.linkedin.com/in/indianutkarsh/
- **Quora:** https://www.quora.com/profile/Utkarsh-Bajpai-82

9 798887 727011

Printed by Libri Plureos GmbH in Hamburg, Germany